If I Were PRESIDENT

WRITTEN BY *Catherine Stier*

ILLUSTRATED BY *DyAnne DiSalvo-Ryan*

ALBERT WHITMAN & COMPANY

MORTON GROVE, ILLINOIS

To every child who aspires to the highest office in the land, and to the possible future presidents in my home, Andrew and Julia. —C. S.

To Kate, Sam, and Mary. —D. D-R.

Library of Congress Cataloging-in-Publication Data

Stier, Catherine.
If I were president / by Catherine Stier ; illustrated by DyAnne DiSalvo-Ryan.
p. cm.
Summary: A simple description of the duties, responsibilities, and traditions of the office of president.
ISBN 0-8075-3541-9
1. Presidents—United States—Juvenile literature. [1. Presidents.]
I. DiSalvo-Ryan, DyAnne, ill. II. Title.
JK517.S75 1999   352.23'0973—dc 21   98-50005
CIP   AC

The art is rendered in acrylics, gouache, and pencil.
The title-page art is by Marja-Lewis Ryan.
The text is set in Bulmer MT.
The design is by Scott Piehl.

TWO UNITED STATES PRESIDENTS, George Washington, the first president, and Abraham Lincoln, the sixteenth, are honored each February on Presidents' Day. But who is the president of the United States, and what does the president do?

The president is leader of the country. Unlike kings and queens, presidents aren't born into the job. The people of the United States choose a president every four years. They vote for the person they want to run their country.

But the president does not run the country alone. According to an important plan called the Constitution, written more than two hundred years ago, a group of people called the Congress make the laws. Other people, called judges, explain the laws.

Some of the president's work is probably fun, such as handing out medals or flying to a meeting in a private jet. But most of the time the president works hard and must think about serious things, like how to spend the country's money and how to get along with other nations. The president helps make new laws and leads America's fighting forces. He (or maybe, someday, she) is also the leader of his political party — usually the Democrats or Republicans.

The Constitution says a person must be born a citizen of the United States and have lived there for at least fourteen years to be president. A person must also be thirty-five years old to hold the highest office in the land. That's it! Perhaps someday *you* may choose — and be chosen — to take on this very important job.

It would be great to be president of the United States!

If I were president, that means after a big campaign with speeches and posters and TV ads, the people would have chosen me as their leader. Years of planning and hard work would have prepared me for that day.

If I were president, I'd promise to "preserve, protect, and defend the Constitution of the United States," because that would be my job.

Then I'd move to a mansion called the White House, with more than one hundred rooms. And I'd have to remember my new address: 1600 Pennsylvania Avenue, Washington, D.C.

If I were president, I could go bowling or visit a movie theater without ever leaving my house.

I'd have my own chef and could eat whatever I wanted.
I could even have two desserts every night!

If I were president, I'd start work early each morning in the Oval Office. Although I'd try to do what's best for my country, not everyone would agree with my decisions.

But I'd get help making those decisions from a group of people called my cabinet.

If I were president, the people would be my boss,
and I'd have to find out what they wanted. It wouldn't be
easy—different people would want different things.

If I were president, I'd be in charge of the armed forces—the army, navy, air force, and marines.

If I were president, each year I'd give a speech to Congress called the State of the Union. All over the country, people would be watching and listening. I'd talk about how our country was doing and suggest ways to solve our problems.

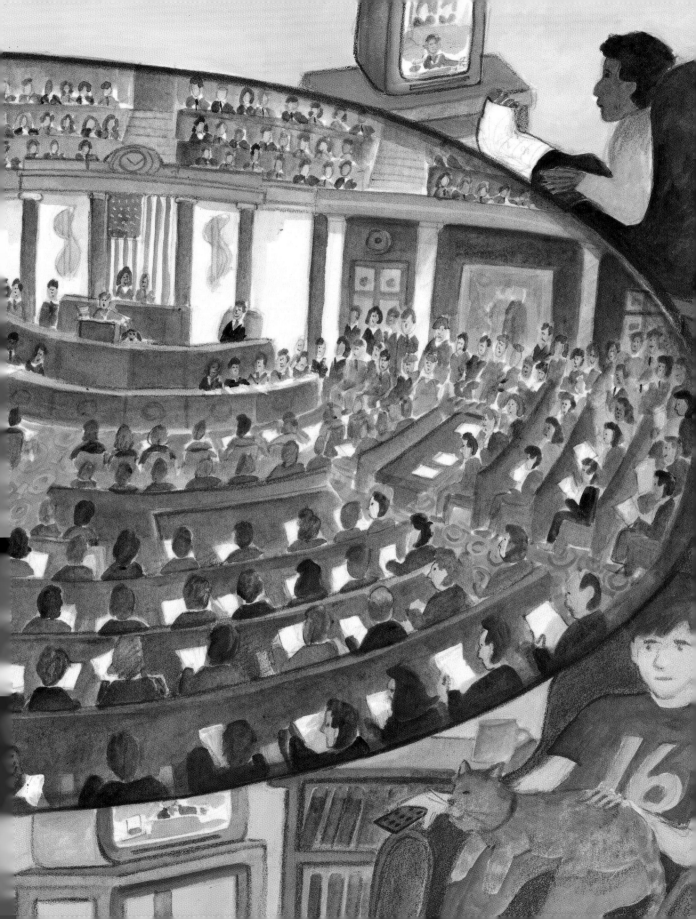

Imagine creating laws for a whole country! That's something Congress and I would work on together. Congress would present bills, which are ideas for new laws. If I didn't like an idea, I'd say no. That's called a veto. But if I agreed, I'd sign the bill and make it a law.

If I were president, the agents of the Secret Service would guard me. Everywhere I'd go, they'd go, too.

If I were president, I'd travel in my limousine or in my own private airplane, Air Force One.

I'd meet with the leaders of other nations. Maybe together we could work to improve our world.

If I were president, I'd comfort families that had been in an earthquake, hurricane, or flood. Then I'd help them rebuild their towns.

If I were president, one of my favorite jobs would be passing out medals to people who had done brave deeds.

If I were president, in the spring I'd toss the first pitch of the baseball season,

and in winter I'd light the nation's holiday tree.

If I were president, my words and picture would appear in newspapers and magazines all over the world.

Even my dog would make headlines!

If I were president, the house I grew up in would be famous.

People would ask my mom for a tour of everything (even my treehouse).

If I were president, the people could only elect me twice—that's eight years altogether. Then I'd have to find a new job and a new house.

Soon a new president, with different ideas, would move into the White House. But just like me, the new president would work hard for the good of the country.

If I were president, they might someday make a statue of me, like the white marble statue of Abraham Lincoln in the Lincoln Memorial, or the presidents' heads carved into Mount Rushmore.

Or someday my face might show up on the country's money. Did you know President Lincoln is on the penny, President Jefferson is on the nickel, and President Washington is on the dollar bill?

And who knows? Someday I just might *be* president of the United States!